Reports
from the
Soul

ROBIN WHITE

ISBN: 979-8-88945-397-0
eISBN: 979-8-88945-398-7

Brilliant Books Literary
137 Forest Park Lane Thomasville
North Carolina 27360 USA

Printed in the United States of America

Contents

Prelude

"Reports From the Soul" is dedicated to Maleah Winter Evans Campbell.

I have gladly walked behind and besides you, to observe your transformation into this remarkable social butterfly, filled with compassion, a safeguard for all as you cry for humanity each time there is a miscarriage of justice. I have great hope for you. It is with sheer pleasure to witness your smile, hear your laughter, to listen to your ideas, to watch you discover multiple forms of life and navigate your way through such a challenging world. I am in your love and it is indeed my pleasure to color you with love.

Baby Cocoa, I am sorry for your early departure from a cold world in which we all failed to protect you. Even so, as a spark of the ancestors, you too are colored with love.

Lisa Collins spent so much time with me while we resided in the Grand Canyon. Our sistership began long before then. I was still a Park Ranger at what was then Indiana Dunes National Lakeshore. I am grateful. For her undeniable faith in me, constantly pushing and encouraging me to bring this book to life. She went so far as to write Oprah Winfrey submitting my story to the "Wildest Dream Come True." This was the moment of revelation for me to self validate!

Thank you nephew D'Hasheem for the love of light you give to nurture my soul, and for the reflection reminding me that I am an image of you. Emory White, thank you for coming to my rescue building me through music and sounding knowledge.

You lifted my spirit with words of encouragement. I commend you for sharing your will of endurance with me after the Wake of Katrina and editing the poetry when my soul was exhausted.

I'd like to thank all the artists for allowing me to work with them and sharing their talents with me. Jim Fuge, James Smith, Ray Skeet, and Charmaine Neville. You brought my harbored words to life with the illustrations; you have the capacity to capture the essence of my soul.

A Believer

I sit with closed eyes; his voice in my ear,
his spirit–in my heart longing for life serenity,
for it is much easier to endure.
Although, the opened Pandora's Box—
causes me to view all the internal pain,
unanswered knocks,
the miscarriage of justice and an explicit part of my voyage
as a recipe for emotional healing.
There is great confidence in knowing
that I don't come from a bad place,
just some damning, difficult times,
like you my needs are the same,
but my experiences are different, and with that….
I am

A BELIEVER

You are revered in the amplitude of mine optic receiver
Your bewitching aura incapacitates me
Absorbed in a sphere of infinite gratification
I am a believer
Reason– irrepressible in an abyss of pleasure
Lay grace on my heart
As we stroll, soul to soul.
Gravitate to the unexplored
In your sacred temple
Inviting, inciting
Ascent– congruent in an uproar
I am a believer

Colored With Love

Often we willfully allow burdens to weigh upon us, creating multiple problems and a fit of dis-ease. Our soul is ragged, and bent from sorrow and worldly battles, although the Creator is universally sovereign, he allows us to make decisions, to make the impossible become possible, so that hopeless becomes hopeful and plentiful. He's our resource, life support, and reservoir in wisdom, spirit and eternity.

As I settle into the comfort of being, it is
imperative to speak from the Queendom within.
The greatest challenge in life is "Knowing" and sitting in
an empty room with your spirit and ability to
differentiate between being lonely and being alone.

Looking out gazing over Grand Canyon,
Multiple images of people and events come to mind, some of those events are on replay, recurring over and over again.

I must give props to the Creator, for he loved me so much that he chose my mother for me to come through, and for that I am most grateful. Although our ways parted in the physical form when I was age eleven; the legacy she left for me to maintain is strong.
She left me deep-rooted in a tapestry of integrity, conditional love, and purpose with the aptitude to endure life's bewildering winds of change. She left with me the will to nurture, cultivate and grow from the inner self.
I remember the harmony of her walk, the cosmos
of her smile, the slight turn of her head, and the
Strength of her back as she held her head so high
I remember the length of her hair that she so easily transformed into a French Bun. The length of her fingers as she patiently taught me to make Hot Water Corn Bread, Smothered Chicken, Mustard Greens and Carmel Cake. I am so fortunate to have come through her as she colored me with love.
So, Yaya if you can hear me
These words are just for you

She has been removed
My heart aches and yearns for more
Of the shadow behind a closed door
The wind will blow her memory around
By the time you remember she won't be found
I don't know why it happened
When I was so far away
But Jah came a calling my Yaya today
I can understand why he wanted a person like her
Poised with dignity so confident and sure
I love you like no other
To me you'll always be
My world navigator
Lifelong educator
You colored me with love

You were my friend
When I thought my world would end
You gave me the love of life
The joy of spice
When I couldn't make the grade
You set wisdom in my shade
You taught me dignity
Underneath the church tree

You colored me with love

I am your offspring, a blooming seed
I know my worth as your dawter
I am of thee a blessing in Jah's creation
You are colored with love

The Chosen Race

The verdict was in long before the jury became blind to the evidence. From childhood I was quite aware of the ways of society. But nothing was as telling as the "Without Sanctuary Exhibit" at Martin Luther King, Jr. National Historical Park in 2003. My breath kept escaping me, my heart ran rapid and my mind screamed never more as I exited the door.

The dark red stains on the trunk
Take us to a place "Without Sanctuary"
Your crumbled body,
soul wrenching scream fell on crazed ears.

As the rope grew tighter, stealing your earthly years,
Not one face spoke of shame, with wild eyes and menacing sneers.
A joyful noise sounded, during their life taking reign.

My heart was heavy, couldn't hold the sight
As your face rapidly swelled,
on this abhorrent lonely night

It is 2023; the stories must be told
As new age Lynching becomes the fatal chokehold.
Countless, senseless; death and loss of hope
our people hung by juries and invisible ropes.

In your darkest hour,
When you defend your case;
What will be your justification
for condemning a chosen race?

Image of You

I come from the bowel of the ancestral dome
Unique skylark guided by the North Star
Seasoned to revolutionize,
Squash tongue twisted lies.
A door of possibility opens each day.
I am what you hear,
I am what you say.
Rules of engagement,
A legend of time.
A Rose unkissed by the dew.
A nod–
A smile–
A scent–
A thought, proposal here and there
A hint of fashion,
Incentive for quota.
I am your advocate, your adversary
Your reason for necessary.
What is now and meant to be
I am hard times, a forgotten eternity.
A rummage round your mind.
The man holding a cup.
Brother screaming Enough is Enough!
Sister looking between the bars
Child reaching for the stars.
I am rules of engagement
A crypt of ancient times.
One ridiculed, scorned, labeled
When in fact I am SABLE!
I am a splinter of fear, wind-probing sound.
A glare of romance, a stolen chance.
I am rules of engagement
A rose unkissed by the dew.
I am an image.
IMAGE OF YOU.....

I Want to Live

Years back while living in Albuquerque, New Mexico
I asked my son, "What do you want for your 13th bornday?"
His reply was " I just want to be alive."
Needless to say, I was quite shocked at his response and as a result dedicated the following to him. This is not just about my son, this is about those gangly teenagers that are coming into their rites of passage and the crossroads are filled with misconceptions, and biases leaving those young men in a vulnerable, confused state of mind. Sometimes they don't get the opportunity to become men, they become statistics.

They assign me the role trouble
Say I'm illiterate because of my skin color
I almost forgot that I am a Prince

They labeled me gangsta
Said I make their schools look bad
They are misinformed people
Hearts of black and eyes of sad
My culture identity, I suffered to maintain
I almost forgot I am a Prince

My color, height and confidence intimidates
My popularity and intelligence infuriates
You release the wrath of hate
Persecute me; dis me; to destroy my faith
I almost forgot I am a Prince

I cannot play the role you delegate
Nor allow you to regulate
Because my clothes are Baggy and my pants sag
This is just a Hip-hop fad
I almost forgot I am a Prince

I strive to get an education
The catalyst of my liberation
I just want to Live to be a KING!

Harbored Words

Words harbor in me,
trapped churning and yearning,
quivering at the base of my being.
Afraid for people to hear my voice, see my thoughts and
become acquainted with the real me.
Expressions struggle to escape.
Seeking refuge in the landscape.
Fundamental in the scheme of things.
what will suppressed words produce?
After years of practiced absence
drifting in a world of borrowed confusion,
words feed on my personification;
lurking stark naked, harboring in me
words forming unshakably,
proposing to set me free.
dare I share?
Or just continue the invisible affair....
Secretly in silence as the world
turns in my mind?

Peace Offering

My elder Rex Tilousi of the Havasupai Tribe in Grand Canyon, Arizona, used to kick knowledge with me as we shared sacred moments together strolling the South Rim of the Grand Canyon.

Sometimes, Rex would say "The Canyon is not happy, she is angry as we take her gifts for granted." My heart is heavy and sometimes I cry for her."

Rex taught me: as we raise our voices in harmony with the echoes of our ancestors, it is a call to our birthright heritage. It is important to preserve our culture so that we can connect with our ancestors in times of yesterday to create a better tomorrow.

I have learned to be still and let the Canyon embrace me; voiced echoes welcome their humble child into an assembly of grandeur. I have learned to stand in silence surrounded by corridors of sound. Mine eyes witness visitors summon strength into trembling legs, shuffling walks, bent backs to meet victory on the last stretch out of the Canyon on to the rim.

I sit still for warmth of different languages that create music in this cathedral, a sacred place for many. The splendor beckons an awakening of overwhelming hunger and life lessons intoxicating my perception, the wind at my back is as a force shifting me into a realm of reality.

I am stilled as I visit the Canyon and other places in my mind's palace, dancing with endless, sojourning upon distance and reaching out to feel expansion. I am witnessing the birth of infinity as colorful buttes across the horizon speak to me. I am stilled as gallant streaks of lightening with flaming colors light up the sky; demanding untarnished silence and respect in view of nature's dauntless sight.

I am transformed as I observe a valley defined by geological time; a place where morning light rises with extraordinary colors that score majestic mountains. I stand on the rim of the Canyon to welcome a kiss from the sun, anticipating multiple sounds, deliberating on the carving nature had done. I am stilled as much is revealed to me in depths, heights, distance, sight, sound, and hue as I venture forth to become me in chambers of light and consciousness.

The Canyon

20

No More Tears

I awoke this morning tired from a restless sleep;
constantly watching the clock waiting for the day to dawn, listening for
another scream, whose turn is it tonight, which family member will have
the Katrina frightmare?

Even though it was fall, the season was dark. I proceeded to prepare for
the day to enjoy the peace while encountering many sounds. My heart
is warmed for I am blessed to rest mine eyes upon N'Awlins relatives
and my ears are blessed to hear their voices. They are not refugees; they
are family, although they are safe, it is hard through personal testimony
witnessing their ordeal. As I moved slowly in a zombie like fashion to
get dressed, once again the compelling need to weep was overwhelming.
My mind relaxed upon family and friends and the many things that we
know to be true.

There is not a day that goes by that family and friends in N'Awlins don't
talk to one another, teach, preach to and love each other. Even though
it is in an impoverished state, the Big Easy is what it is because of the
people. My heart was warmed because I could hear their voices, smell
them, touch them and hold them to ease our pain.

Several family members experienced unspeakable atrocities. A dear friend
was interviewed by People Magazine, and during the interview Champ
said " I have no more tears to cry." Champ', Cousin Doris, LaWanda, Z,
and I talked every other day, and we cried like women warriors, not for
the souls that are gone home, but for the way they went home, for those
that turned their back on the people, and for the day that the Creator
will show his hand. Out of the shadow of my people I stand as a voice
for my ancestors.

I keep hanging on to goodness, disregarding the obstacles. I look out
into the world searching for a piece of me, trying to understand how
intrusive obstacles fit into the scheme of things, tenaciously bucking up
against the full weight of trying to close the broken circle.

The thought of I ain't crying no more sits at the bottom rising like a light throughout the Queendom within. With noble intentions, the mental images rid the soul of emptiness, as the Creator becomes the central figure of my life.

Despite what one has learned, as I marinate in the will of endurance, I can't help but to hate my life at times. Often the scream is as useless as an education, as pointless as determination, for I am invisible, unseen, unwanted and unheard. But I am comforted because I ain't crying no more.

As the seed of dreams spiral into an abyss of hopelessness and despair, somehow I still manage to care and muster an ounce of humanity towards my earthly siblings. The self doubt is discarded like old news and the inside rage that keeps us beholden in bondage is no longer my burden to bear.

Struggling against the circumstances that transform the incomplete life, and braving to dwell in the valley of sprouted memories that give birth to harmonious times; the speed of victories run rapid in mine mind. I exit the place of gated communities and padlocked doors to claim fame and peace in the galaxy once ridden before. I move with the stars and yield to embrace my spirit because the AGREEMENT is made that I ain't crying no more!

We are born into a circle of family and friends, which is our birthright heritage. However, it is up to us to keep that bond and invest in our future generations. Family is ABSOLUTE!

No More Tears................continued

New Orleans as of January 2007

New Orleanians are a people embedded in rich cultural traditions whose lives have been reduced to spoils of despair.

In 2005, the 3, 4, 5, 6, 7, 9, 13 and 17 Wards were filled with the spirit of a people steadfast realizing their dreams.

Once upon a time neighborhoods from New Orleans East, St. Bernard Parish, Treme, Gert Town, Up Town, Gentily, Central City, Bayou St., John, Magnolia, Desire, and Lafitte Housing Developments were flowing with life. Music, Red Beans & Rice, Crawfish Boils defined and added value to the communities.

Today, New Orleans is a city trying to resurface from the assault of the broken levees, and abandonment.

The abandonment is real with broken hearts and dreams as generations of memories lay in ruins, and our people die in epidemic numbers.

You can feel the lingering quiet desperation. But we are a proud people, true warriors that are diligently rising slowly from the mounds of debris that just so happen to represent personal life stories.

New Orleans as of February 2007

I want you all to understand that everything is not all right in New Orleans. You see, life legacy of our bloodline is ordained before birth. As born ambassadors of our bloodline we are welcomed into a circle of family and friends similar to clans. New Orleanians are cultivated like everyone else for their true destiny and when one falters under the enormity of life there is family.

Of course this no longer rings true for most New Orleanians today, as generations are scattered afar, some lost, mind distorted, and culture destroyed. How do you unlearn the learned value of community? I read about the crime and the negative attributes of New Orleans. However, I am yet to read about the courage of our next social guards. Our youth are the future of this country, and they are trying to maintain what they have been taught about community. We cannot see their sheer will to hold on to their dreams, and culture as they strive to be normal during un-normal times. Our beautiful innocent children are determined to get an education, and as a Council of Elders it is our responsibility to uplift them. Their determination and maturity are boundless as they attend schools that lack sufficient supplies to nurture their minds. Interfacing directly with the unwarranted assault is undeniable unjustifiable. It is heart wrenching witnessing the rape of a people, as if they need permission for existence. My spirit is bent with unrest!

I Know Your Kind

Our greatest dead beat dads are our founding fathers who planted seeds of biblical proportions all over the world, and yet, we overlook, and excuse their misdeeds even though they cunningly created the behavior.

You don't wanna hear what I have to say
Nodding your head turning your eyes away
Because I speak the truth
Peeling the layers off you
What's buried underneath
Can make the devil weep

A biological default of lies and deception
Misrepresentation
The undesirable rests deep within thee
Lots of shaking the infidelity tree

You don't wanna hear what I have to say
Bite your lips turn your face away
Because I have knowledge of the suspect
The abortions, the secret intoxication
The unschooled and the blaxploitation

You strive to hide
Lies that swim in your eyes
Darkness that lurks in your heart
You lie in wait for another soul to take
The seed of misery
Immured in dishonesty
Can smell your wrenched life rankness

You don't wanna hear what I have to say
Shaking your head walking away
Seen you exercise your right to capitalize
I know the real deal
Predator going for a kill
The beauty, innocence and richness of another
Spit out uncharted quibbling
Running a course to deceive sisters and brothers

The fool, wanna be; the imprudent lover
You were not born of a woman
You were hatched of another

Sour Soul

Your demise is the failure to recognize that I've no use for constrictive
sour souls.

I do not like your vibes.
They pronounce jive.
Wandering in unannounced, the opportunist ready to pounce
Plastered upside frown,
as if I want you in my world.
I do not like your eyes,
Hooded and gloomy
You have a sour soul.

You have a Bachelor in brutality,
put the C in cunning
A Master in manipulation
you throw bad vibrations
Graduate street fool, I do not like you.

I do not like your hands.
They are hard as your heart.
You have a sour soul

Talk about righteousness and free,
Eclipse of misrepresentation
Armed with diseases of society,
I refuse to let you infect me.
You have a sour soul.
I really do not like you.

Our History

They say "the land of the Free," I guess the world is blind to the truth.
Remember in history rhymes? In 1492, Columbus sailed the ocean blue?
Glorified mass murder; as I ramble further through history, way back;
I discovered some of the first drive-bys were committed on horse back.
straight up annihilated tribal Indian nations,
Invaded Africa continent for sport, sexual recreation
and pirating gratification.
Created reservations our ancestors' blood stained the nation
from encampments and plantations; while mutilated for sensations,
and mass marketed enslavement.
After four hundred years of Black Holocaust denied reparations
I call them the Danger Gangster
Refined BAR B ARIC
Through their God taken rights
Knight Riders, White Supremacy the Klan
Rule with hate
Rule with murder and mayhem
Rule with guns
Rule with bombs
Rule with drugs
Rule the economy
Notorious thug
Sweet land of liberty and free
I call them the Danger Gangster
Look at our history.
Dreams deferred and aborted,
Land of transplantation,
of the transported.
We ain't in Recession.
We in session of America genocide
and global oppression.
Who dictates to the people?
Own our mine,
Own our time,
Who cripple planes?

Bring stereo into radios.
Make television tunnel vision.
Plant seeds of hate.
Through their radical dictate.
The Danger Gangster
Where is Medgar, What happened at Wounded Knee?
Where are Martin, Malcolm, and Garvey?
What happened to Crazy Horse, Sitting Bull, Black Elk, Che,
Fannie Lou, and our Four Little Girls, who tells the untold,
Who conquers, and divides
Who is riding the tide on American Apartheid?
In the land of the free
Is this the way of democracy or the Danger Gangster?
Who can do the do with no one to answer to?
Who is the director of evil invent?
Who implemented the Tuskegee experiment?
Who is the thief of all thieves?
Expert of disguise who stole everything that we created
Define us, define you
Ingeniously create laws
Command what we can and cannot do.
Can you name the Danger Gangsters
who sell us lies encased in hardback books?

They try to convince me and my people that this is the land of the free;
Like there is totally no existence of our-OUR HISTORY!

Invisible Man

As I was bringing life into this world, my father Johnny White crossed over. A cloud of drunkenness overshadowed his existence as he struggled to be invisible. We didn't converse much, yet, as a child I knew the depths of his soul. I felt his sorrow, and his undeniable pain.

Maybe I didn't overstand all that was revealed to me. But with certainty, I held on to the rememories of the making of this man. Overcoming the challenges of living on a plantation and making it through World War II were no small tasks.

During a walkabout through Shaw in D.C.
He shuffled past me with crooked legs and bowed head.
Something from him was drawing on me;
Rememories of time, hands held by another

A dark silhouette stuttering "dis, dis, dis my dawter".
Strolling down 2-5 in the City of GI (Gary, Indiana).
she catches a glimpse of a soul that captures her time.
Hunched shoulders, smell of urine, and crouched real low,
the man who wants to be invisible,
reminds her of another with the Frederick Douglas Afro.

One day in M. C. (Michigan City), Indiana down the back alley she goes.
She hears angry shouts, and noted cruel words fall on the drunken man

Screaming and tearing through the circle in a rage,
stricken by unknown pain she dares anyone to come forth and engage
To others her bold actions speak of one insane.

All the while the lioness child protects the drunken man.
One questions who is he to you?
He is just a drunken fool

With raining eyes of pride and heart of sadness
gently gripping the hand of the drunken man.
Undeterred and unashamed, she screamed "dis, dis, dis MINE DAD"!

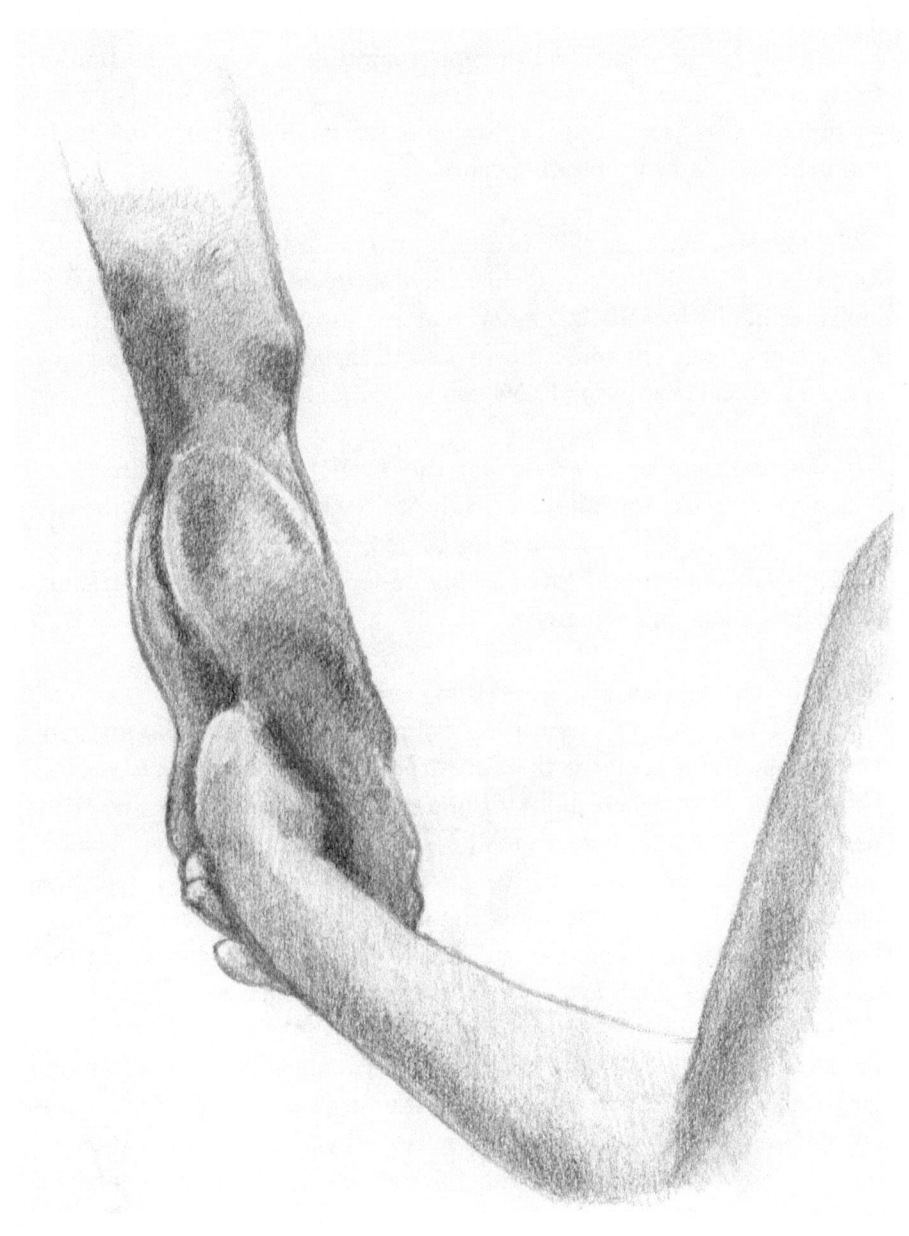

The Border

There was a time in my life when I felt safe, secure, and the neighborhood yaya's in the village had say in my upbringing. I loved the Border because we all knew one another. It was strongly family oriented even though some bad seeds were beginning to penetrate our harm-free environment and challenge our innocence.

12345678910, wheeeew !!!!!!, pause to catch your breath, sing 11 12 13 14 15 16 17 18 19 20, lean against the doorframe, turn the knob, door ain't ever hardly locked. A wonderful aroma captures you. Ain't nothing like coming home to some brown stew Chicken, Hopin Jon and hot water cornbread; 'cause you know you are in a soulful home.

My favorite piece of furniture was the kitchen table. Her name was Maelee, lookin' like she's fit for a family of fifteen instead of nine. She sits up right high as if she's royalty; leg bowed, with knobbed feet, getting ready to run at anytime. I loved sitting under Maelee and watch friends and families legs and feet go by.

Maelee was the center of everything and knew everybody's secrets. You see, I was always on punishments for doing crazy shit and my only form of entertainment was the diningroom table and picture windows. During my down time I didn't sit in a corner. I'd dress Maelee up with fancy cloth, lay under her and tell her all my troubles. I call her Maelee because almost everybody in the family are named Mae or Lee. She didn't talk back just let me know that everything would be all right by her strong presence. That's how I learned to be still and listen to the noise, sometimes when I'm alone I can hear the silence too.

In the family room, my favorite place was the looking glass. Down on the far corner of the block was the neighborhood store. Everybody says the owner is nice cause he a Jew. All I see is a round Buckra who pat us on our head and backside all the time. I think a Jew is somebody that let all the black kids work in his store.

In the middle of the block is Ruthie's Place. Everybody be at Ruthie's to play those machine games, the music box, eat the best, greasiest burgers in town. They were better than King Kastle and Coney Island burgers. I loved to watch people dance and would often join in to show the older kids the latest dances. Horse and KJ would sit outside and breathe in bags all day. I say to mine self, "one day I'm gonna buy me some air to breathe in those paper bags when I get big".

The other looking glass gave me witness to the light skinned family across the street, with good hair and dimples in their faces. Three of them girls are always together holding hands. The oldest one constantly wants me to give mine brother love messages from her. He be right there, why don't she tell him herself?

A holler down the street from the three girl's house was a huge girl named Teenie. There wasn't a damn thing Teenie or Tiny about her, so I called her Baby Huey. I be thinking people better move, she look like she gonna bust wide open on somebody. She just waddles from side to side and breathes hard. I don't think no store got draws her size.

I wonder how her feet carry that big ole body?

Next door to us was a house filled with women. I thought they were just a big ass family of girls. People were whispering about them all the time, say they "ladies of the night". We been warned by all the neighborhood yaya's not to go near them no good women. They for sure going to hell. It's amazing how you can look at folks and tell if they are going to hell. I guess some of us got the hook up with God more so than others.

They look like normal women to me in the daytime: course; I ain't seen how they look at night. One day I heard mine Yaya fussing at mine sister about being around those fast women and how lucky she was to be in God's grace. One of those unfortunate women was found murdered in a hallway. I asked God, who wanna hurt those ladies? All they do is smile at you and wear funny clothes.

They call this area the Border; I say Buckras don't know everything. Ain't nothing bored about this place, something always happens on either corner or around the corner. Why come every time a police car turns the corner everybody runs? You learn to run from the police at an early age, and it don't make any difference if you a girl or boy. Folks got it all wrong 'cause I sho don't see nothing bored on the Border.

Family's Enemy Friend

Although I was born in the North, I was married to the South in some strange way. After several family crises, school was no longer a priority, and during my early adolescent years I roamed the Delta, trying to find my niche. Family was glad to see me in New Orleans, Louisiana and Schlater, Mississippi. Although my presence brought some unwanted ghosts to surface in Schlater, Mississippi.

Her mind was fixed on finding Pokeweed as she strolled down the dirt road. She mentally noted how her return caused such pandemonium. The whispers, "You and the other one are about the same age. You could be twins' alike, 'cept you court darker skin".

Much confusion in their words of warning till the day she happened upon the family's enemy-friend. There he rocked back and forth, older than olden, skeletal hands beckoning her near, she froze as her eyes took in her family's fear. He looked like everyone's grandpa or great grand-papa, thin as a willow, the ancestor whispered "Beware child for he is strong and fit".

So much family legend, no, he can't be the same, the one they laid blame on for fixing my sister in her youthful years. Unafraid and filled with anger, their eyes locked and she then knew that this was the man that cursed her sister Lois. He called her by the name of the other one. The family's enemy friend stood half bent and tears flowing down his weathered worn face as he sought absolution for his earthly sins. She stood in agony hearing the name of the other fall repeatedly from his lips.

Realizing why Jah brought her to this place, knowing it was destiny to meet the family's enemy-friend. She was the same age as the other; people testified that they looked twin-like. Ole man Judd begged her for forgiveness, unaware of the darker skin.

Some years back, surrounded by the ancestors, a girl child was summoned to exonerate the sins of her family's enemy-friend

Dedicated to my sister

41

The Visitor

I felt something drawing on my energy, as I tried to sleep. It pulled me deeper and deeper as I loudly screamed. Nobody heard me nor came to my rescue as the grievous screams were released from my soul. This happened three nights in a row. Upon returning home I began to make phone calls to check on the well being of family members. It was then that I learned that my cousin crossed over without any warning. I knew that she came to visit me and I was too afraid to listen.

The rain came down cleansing the earth
Tuesday night, while in quest of slumber
at the charming Sulphur Springs Inn, Oklahoma
a visitor, unseen to me was within
taxing presence; messing with my mind
interrupting my dreams.
Image tossing, body freeze, brain squeeze.
None heard the ghastly screams
escaping from the constricted voice box,
mind reeling, body dispirited
doors locked, unanswered knocks.
Stumbling, grasping for security,
tried to shake, couldn't break the hold.
Mine visitor dragged me deeper and deeper
Mind wrapped around the Creator!!!
Ancestors summoned with all mine strength!!
Energy blast at last!
The unwanted is dispatched
Am I free........?.
As I rise weary and fatigued,
From wrestling with a visitor,
I failed to let communicate with me.
Am I free..........?.

Lil Black Boy

One day in early 2002, my grandson came home from Day Care in Grand Canyon, AZ and asked me "what is a nigga"? I put my heart in check, but the rage was about to tip me over, and I asked why? He said "cause "they call me that and I don't like the way it sounds grandma, the word feels like something real bad". How do you help a five year old understand? How do you tell your children how warped the world is, and it's not their fault? How do you prepare them for what is to come?

Hey! lil black boy come down near.
I got some words for your earthly years.
You will be called trouble maker
have conflict with heart breaker
be labeled instigator
befriend the local undertaker
as you step unto the killing fields.

Hey! lil black boy sit your bottom down.
Let me introduce you to true and sound.
You will get a degree titled "lessons in trickery".
You'll feast on books authored by crooks.
as institutions rape your mind
You'll court confusion, sex up illusion.
graduate on tasteful lies.

Hey! lil black boy come down near
I got some wisdom for your ears.
Walk proud, court your culture unashamed,
offset their political games.
You are the offspring of higher kingdoms,
seed of a true civilization.

Damn

In route of a better way
There you were hiding in plain sight
On the long hard road
Of spiritual confusion
Never once did I doubt
Such a beast that kills
With thrusts of illusion
So charming and disarming
Incredible sensations
Trepidation seized the imagination
Victim of a bad relation
Your generosity defied description
Reliable, undeniable
Unsuspecting of the suspect
That kept me in check
In a strange land
Operating under a foreign command
Impotent mind in another place
Engineered the motion of change
Like quick sand
Suffocate all that you can
Yet, I loved you
All I knew to be true
Surfaced as multiple lies
Reduced to a stench in the gutter
Damn.......
Drugs are a Mother Fucker!

Have You Ever Seen A Silent Scream?

Going back yonder wasn't all that hard I carry good and bad memories. I am stock of mine people and while most of them were raised in the Southern way, I just wasn't so eager to adhere to the lifestyle of the South. The most frequent words thrown at me was, "come here you lil ole nappy head geeche. "Now, at that time I didn't rightfully know what they were calling me. However, I knew it was nothing nice for the Buckras to be calling me that. Times were hard even on children.

I used to wonder why we called our Grandyaya Lilbit? Today, I know it was because that's all she had to give, was a lil bit of love, a lil bit of food and a lil bit of herself. Wasn't much room in those places called shacks (shotgun houses). There were empty rooms with unrecognizable furniture, overflowed with people. When you found a bed it was filled with bodies, arms across faces, legs across hips, bodies of all shapes, and colors and musty smells.

I didn't get to know my grandyaya much as a child and didn't get to overstand her as I got older. I do know she loved her some liquor and she loved men even more. She had a whole lot of babies for them. Two sets as I recollect, my daddy was of the first set.

You see, I didn't think much of growing up on a plantation. It seemed fitting to do whatever I wanted since all my kinfolk were picking cotton. They tell me I had a mind of mine own that was no good and was just going to get me in real trouble or killed. It irritated the hell out of me to step off the sidewalk for those good folks! If they were such good folks then what that made us?

Folks say it ain't natural for a child to run wild like that. I say it ain't natural to be found frozen to death, naked in the summertime. They think I don't know about Uncle Bopeep. I know and I'm still pretty damn mad. I say it ain't natural to take a human being, and cut them up like sausage only to deliver him to his people.

How many silent screams can a family endure?

Aunt Louise always going around giving people a piece of her mind. One day her cup runneth over, her mind left her never to be found again. They say Bright Eyes crazy cause she don't know who she is. I say she just all twisted up inside cause she got one green eye and one brown eye. She take the green eye out cause people be messing with her. Don't make no difference everybody knows who child she be. Sometimes it don't make no sense to know who you are, cause you are not going to like yourself anyway. Some folks just born to be miserable the rest of their lives.

I tell you what I do know today. I love mine people, they are the most beautiful, courageous people you are blessed to meet. You see mine fore-fathers and mine father raised the children that were the rape of their wives. They were the strong and silent type and just let the rage flow through them. Have you ever seen a silent scream?

I can never know mine yaya's and baba's pain. I could never walk in their shoes, or carry the humiliation they carried with such dignity. Yet, they stood tall as an oak. These are mine memories of back yonder. Then one day, I witnessed the silent scream. Life took mine grandyaya Lilbit and doubled her over, and she took what life dealt out to her. Yeah, she took it and began to live in a bottle.

Don't Call Me

In every yard there is potential for growth, every cemetery an artist, and in every society there are those who create chaos and mayhem upon their loved ones. How do you divorce yourself from such overwhelming tribulations? One day I looked in the soul of a friend and noted it was absent, and I had no choice but to clearly make her understand "Don't Call Me At All."

Don't call me Sista
While you manipulate and dictate
How to corrupt my younger sistas and brothas.

Don't call me brotha
While you scheme and groan
Taking my younger brothas and sistas on trips
To the twilight zone.

Don't call me Mother
While you steal from
And kill the next brotha man
After you come out of church
And start your negative shit again.

Don't call me friend;
While you lust for my father, brotha, and family belongings
While you lie and cheat your way, out all of our lives

Don't call me at all!

Indigo Man

You are the ancestral calling,
as they rise to speak the spoken.
You are the song of the voices
denied human rights and life choices

Speak, spoken, speak Indigo
The spoken word begins from the
breath of the ancestors.
As you stand in truth,
honoring them with libations.

Speak, spoken, speak Indigo
You are the calm in the man-invented storms.
Indigo long ago kidnapped, and
transplanted across the transatlantic
in a strange place

Speak, spoken speak Indigo
Damned by reason of your race
No matter. You survive
through their schemes and lies.
They kill three and another comes.

Speak, spoken speak Indigo.
You are the descendant of great ones.
You are the spoken word they have not heard,
nor seen Zora's dust tracks on the road;
or met Langston's Jess Simple.

Speak, spoken speak Indigo.
Do they know our Native Son?
You shall not be outdone.
You are the whisper of the spoken,
living by the word Indigo.

Speak, spoken speak Indigo
Put your lips on me and blow Satchmo.
You are the Rhapsodies in motion
melodies across many oceans

Indigo is not a token.
We know you as spoken.
Rising above the trees
Used leisurely to lynch thee.
Speak, spoken, speak Indigo.

You beat chain gang blues,
rescued sister Sarah,
crossed Mississippi's Killing Fields,
mowed down the reign of Sugar Canes,
Infused with the sounds of Africa.
Speak, spoken, speak Indigo

In Honor of My Yayas

In the African American community we have many First Ladies. We children knew that there were universal mothers who lived beyond our neighborhoods. Royalty was my yaya's birthright. You see, her back was always straight and her head held so high as if she was conversing with the creator, as she moved with mother earth, her motion was in tune with everything surrounding her.

Our Yayas' were the pillars of the communities; they were our teachers, our cornerstone. They were change agents and while sitting and watching my yayas' in action I observed and absorbed as much as I could stand. One who teaches must also learn. If I am to share, I must learn to be humble and live with all those surrounding me.

"Where there is a woman there is magic. If there is a moon falling from her mouth. She is a woman who knows her magic. Who can share or not to share her powers" –Ntozake Shange, Sassafras, Cypress and Indigo

Not many words can so grandly describe the First Ladies that I carry closely in my hope chest. I am beholden to those who braved the weary paths slaying the dragons of ornery vipers.

The valley is much deeper as the likes of renowned vocalist Marion Anderson,
socially conscious Josephine Baker,
integrationist Daisy Bates.
educator Mary McCleod Bethune,
gospel recording artist Mahalia Jackson,
writer Audre Lourdes,
educator Dr. Betty Shabazz,
photographer Homai Vyarawalla,
entrepreneur Maggie Walker, civic activists Ida B. Wells, leave us a legacy to maintain.

Moreover, there is the gentle radiance of those today that I uphold to fuse with mine. I give honor to Yaya Maya Angelou,
Angela Davis,
Ruby Dee,
Oprah Winfrey,
Nikki Giovanni,
Lena Horne,
Coretta Scott King,
Wilma Mankiller, and Mah Jong Orphan.

Sometimes I hear words such as 'courage' ringing in my ears, and witness earnest words such as 'integrity' drip off once tight closed lips. And I see words such as 'sanctuary' forming in the mind of others, taking shape in their hearts, tracing limbs and reaching across centuries circling around Fannie Lou Hamer, just embracing her form and filling her with love and I yearn for sisterhood. My smile is warm and wide because I have seen my First Ladies and have lain some of them to rest.

We are what we have learned from all those who have taught us, in the face of hopelessness. I am here to tell you that we cannot enter a door without the sacrifice of those who came before us. And I sing for our Mothers cause they speak in their walk, their clothes, their eyes, their times of lean; they speak in silent voices and create the unseen. The magic in their stories is not what they have done, but what they are yet to do.

My foremothers are the reservoir of dreams, from grand delusions of insular solutions, protectors of the kill of a dubious world with veiled truths. They are the keeper of wisdom untold. The motion that moves others to be, the sweet sound of music, the eloquence in poetry.

Everywhere we go, we are a communal part of the universe. We were part of September 11, 2001. We were part of the Western Fires, the Southeast Hurricanes; we were part of Tsunami 2004, for we are one with the universe. What effect groups in one part of the country impacts us everywhere.

Where Are My Brothers?

Where are my Brothers of natural wealth?
Buffed in cinnamon, chocolate, honey coated armor
dark olive brown
sensual skin, soulful sin?

Disclose yourselves, brothers
Black and blue
Tried and true
Where are you?

Where are my brothers - dream makers
Body rolled real tight
Stimulating, rousing my appetite?

Where are my brothers with soup cooler lips?
Baptized in Java make a sista wanna holler!!
Where are my brothers to ease my pain

Where are my brothers, strong in mind?
Know the joy of living
Gift of giving?

Where are my Prophets?
My Drum Majors
My Gladiators
My Universal Stars
My Martyrs
My Shit Starters?

Where are my brothers of flair?
Eyes of melody
Hands rock a soul free
Lips that promise infinity

Where is that man?
Where are my kinsmen?
My Black-Afro-AMERICAN
King of Kings!

Dance Denied

We procrastinate, and put off responsibilities. The denied dance is an option. We have choices. And can choose not to stay in unwanted relationships, be it work; church; friendships, and family or supposedly a soul mate. I am the captain of my ship and refuse to settle for anything less. How about you?

A dance denied.
Broken up inside
you sit in fester
chasing yesteryear urban jesters.
Committed to life long semesters,
of no soul dance.
Glommed rooms, polluted affairs, and vacant stares.
Visions of penetrations, and stimulating conversations,
for lack of body sensations and mind recreation.
A dance denied.
Locked down inside.
What would you be, if not for the chains of society?
Sporting designer racial jackets,
yeah, you paid for that package.
Do you wanna dance?
Do you wanna take a chance?

Back in the Day

He was my first true love.
And I am honored for his role in my life.
because he contributed--to my liberation
of growing in and out of love with him.
There are no desperate measures to capture a man,
because I am satisfied knowing what love is
for I have once experienced the art and beauty of love
It was good!
I can't wait to explore, discover; nurture and taste it again,
but there are no desperate measures.

He called late in the day
just to touch base
Wanted to hear mine voice,
laughed and teased me about how I can
butcher the English language.
Needed a friend he said, to revisit old times,
Lonely--Missed back in the day
He wants to know do I still dance,
loved to watch me dance
Do I still twist my lips,
loved that crooked dimpled smile.
He said, "when I bat mine eyes people are in trouble.
Don't miss that!"
Missed watching me stroll,
know mine stroll anywhere.
He apologized for his wayward ways.
He is sorry, misses me so much.
I feel his pain, hear his pain,
not doing drugs anymore he says.

My heart is so heavy,
once you go forward you can't go back.
I grew up, moved on, and he moved out.
He is still my strength to this very day.
Although he is with the ancestors,
so far away and yet so near,
I can hear every word that he wants to say.
I am a better person because of Back in the Day!

Finding Your Voice

Every basic relationship involves the engagement of another. When the sun creeps past the leaves, and top the tree branches off with its glory, rising; seeping through the blinds entering my room, gently gliding over my frame; towering over my bed to greet me, I am enraptured with God.

A sense of spirit is in all of us; it begins with embracing your beliefs in spite of the craziness that surrounds you. When you place yourself in a position to grow you trust everything at face value, living with premium purpose and accepting others in their own evolution. There is balance in all things and with that one must lean on her own overstanding flourishing on goodness and dining on integrity. My bloodline will suffer erroneously if I spend lengthy periods of time as a negaholic, victimizing myself from the table adorned with self-hatred and bitterness. My journey through the habitation of mine mind will help me bring forth peace from my inner core.

I am a product of the life ways of those who came before me, those imbued in wisdom, bent with courage and the will to survive. I am my mother's daughter, my father's offspring, the conception of great seeds. I am a provider of customer service to our family and friends, a broker of conditional love. And I play a vital role in fostering stewardship of trust, universal values, and cultivating potential seeds in my loved ones.

While lying in the comfort of my canopy bed, worldly problems run through my mind. I've met so many people with dismembered spirits and broken dreams over the past few months. I am most fortunate to have the Creator lift me when my convoluted spirit causes me to fall. The creator lightens the burden that contributes to body trauma whenever I call on him. Many times I wavered; and blamed others for my tribulations instead of looking at my life plight as unveiled befalling. Even in darkness there is greatness and something from my family lineage is drawing on me, pulling me; pushing me onward to survive.

During my alone times conversing with the creator, appraising my daily routine there is joy and reason to pause. Only when I am consciously awake do I learn something from every individual sent into my life. For so long I was lost like night fading into day with damned dreams, faint hope and my soul involuntarily drifting away. The Creator loves me for whom I am, constantly challenging and calling me to awareness. I inhabit a world of excessive hate, silent screams, forfeited laughter, deprived living, rivers of tears and unconditional love industriously seeking my true birth purpose.

I relinquish any specter of thought that causes me to think I have control over the life of others. I have no answers and instead of asking why, I ask why not, instead of complaining my motto is "I can't complain."

Let Me Into You

Baaaaby, open your chamber of emotions
As I enter your heavenly cascades
and bring forth a realm of passion.
Let me dine on love conditionally
Let me,
Let me into you!
Receive me with a peaceful sigh.
moving from the tightness and seriousness of self
Let me,
Let me into you!
While we dance the sensations,
of sensuous wealth.
Fingers walk ----bodies talk
Lips finesse a pearl of caress
that induces ripples of orgasms
illuminating our oneness.
Let me,
Let me into you.......

Dem Dar Eyes

Body afflicted with a degree of urgency
Dem dar eyes
Conveys a sexy dialogue
Seduced in a crowd
Silence loud and intense
Sauté with happiness
Heavenly induced with a look
Aura got me hooked
Don't know what is real
Luscious way to feel
Ignite a fire inside
Smoldering concocting naughty notions
Give way to a wreck effect
Plant the seed
I am yours to feed
Dem dar eyes
Seize me captive
On a crowded street
Our souls ascend to meet
Fingertips longing to stroke
Dark wet lips
Pour me over you
Wear me like a body suit
Dem dar eyes calling
Softly commanding
The essence of this candy

You Are Weighed

On this blessed day, the rest of our lives begin.
We come together, as friends, to merge, soul-mated,
husband and wife.
I've pledged to be your life-time by standee
In the role of passion and the drama of love.
Without measure, you are weighed, forever in my heart
May your fingerprints petition every portion of me;
as we bond together as lock and key;
to feast upon a menu of life, hopes and dreams.
A space and time of Kings and Queens
Without measure, you are weighed
Forever in my heart

All That I Knew

We loved hard—
stronger than a double addict.
Our love was big.
He constantly made room for my family,
for they were always in need.
When we met at the killing floor
it started– up against the wall.
It was deeper than the skin,
it was to the bone.

Last night his strong hands pulled me to him
Announcing the wanting of my sacred temple
His incredible soft lips were everywhere
Chasing the daily pain away
His arms enfold mine body
Unto his fortress of love
His hands molded, urgently massaged mine breast,
Mine back, mine onion, mine thighs
His fat fingers slowly traveled in search of my triangle of love

His enchanting hands serenading mine body
His low moans against mine neck, on mine belly button.
The heavy breathing was galvanizing

I took him in with mine eyes that witnessed
The torrent of love consume him
He filled the room and all that I knew was him
All that I heard was him
Mine hip did a slow grind against his backside
His manhood throbbed, standing erect
He reached back, and pulled me closer
for more up against the wall love

My performance called for me to face mine opponent

Lawd, loving like dis is just a sin
We engaged and dined on one another
Married in several positions
Hips locked, bodies rocked
Dancing the dance of sweet romance
And then his gripping embrace
Muffled moans told me when

All that I knew was him
All that I saw was him
All that I heard was him
as mine man fell into a deep, drug like sleep

Prescription

I have some of the most beautiful dark skinned nieces and cousins. Two of my nieces are ebony and elegant although they fail to see the beauty of their soul. All they see is a dark skinned woman, with enlarged lips, long necks and legs. I compliment the young women on their beauty and gracefulness at every opportunity. It's a damn shame at how many people think that their dark skin is a sin to the point of self-hatred and suicide. Being the open minded person that I am, when a dark skinned brother crosses my path it is my duty to let him know how beautiful he is, the phrase going something of this nature "You are one dark fine-ass brother, " and just walk away.

Cast your blessings upon me kinsmen, as I drink in your historical shades and hues
Chocolate, cocoa, red, brown, black and blue.
I want your brilliance meandering with mine
As you polish me with a look, that brings into being the fullness of self
Fine Mr. Divine,
Your disposition is heartfelt.
Passionate eyes deep as the sea
invoke rapture in me
Where is my fearless hero?
I am your lesson, what you need to know
Can you get with this flow?
My King,
with impressionable full lips,
Taste my smile, from one corner to the other.
Valorous walk, audacious gaze....a prescription for the mission
Voice that suggests, penetrates minds, shudder spines
Roll with the best
Epitome of intellect

Emancipate Me

You arrest me
Long to be your need
Hearing inner voice
Speak of that which
Make eyes moist
Emancipate me!
Heard your voice
Tasted your thoughts
Dream of you in my sacred place
As I savor your lips
Memories are kind
Emancipate me
The echo of your sigh
Haunt my thighs
Traveled to a much deeper place
Where we succumbed
To the beat of drums
Rememories
Conjured up free
In a sphere beyond hopeless dreams
Living, lying and dying
Emancipate me
As I sip on your sweetness
Inebriated by your deepness
Want to know your masculine edge
Feel you breathe through my chest
As we surge and merge
Emancipate me

Soft Approach

Immersed in chocolate covered passion,
Cover me with your soft approach.
Loving, giving ways, dark bedroom eyes
Releasing the man within thee

Movements manifest the strength of a panther.
Come forth to make your claim.
Disclose buried emotions.
Penetrating, and rippling,
through your aroused stature frame, piercing your soul
Convey an instrument used to rid me of the rage, passion and pain
percolating inside me;
As we move to the rhythmic pulse racing through our veins.
Indulge in my inviting, comforting apparel
Come to me.
Know you are safe,
as I slowly mount the throne to receive you.
Granting you the pleasure of entering my,
corridors of succulent lasting tenderness

Our communal will afford you mounds of joy, and opportunities of
immense eruptions
Cover me with your Soft Approach!

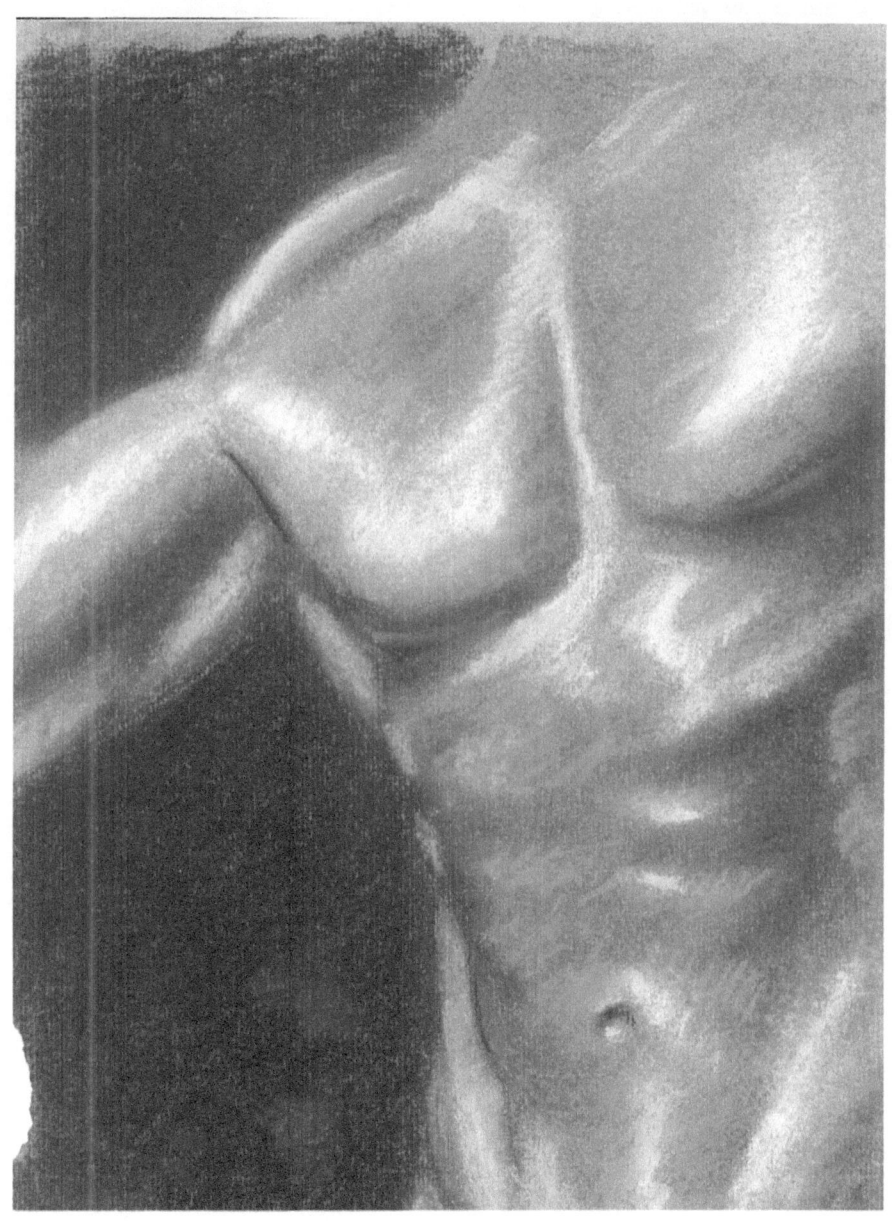

Reflections

I look at you and see me,
trying to snatch the label off we.
"She is too militant, too aggressive they said,
Too dark and nappy bout the head".
Buckras eye shift when I come around, turn up their noses, thinking
cruel thoughts.
I can teach these fools shit they ain't never thought about
My sashay speaks regal.
My mind says I'm lethal.
I am a sister of the universe,
Dawter of the stars.
No, I don't know shit about mars.
But, I can tell you about plantation education.
I can school you on the degradation of segregation.
The star spangled banner don't mean shit to me.
It doesn't symbolize my history.
Daisy Mae, Johnnie Mae, Sylvia Mae, Versie Mae and Bobbie Ree
enlightened me.
I learned those damn books are full of deceit and disloyalty.
I have my yaya's mind; I'm sharp as a whip.
I have my baba's high cheekbones and full ripe lips.
The wannabe imitators that are really perpetrators,
Whisper, "she's too black, back water geeche-girl".
But I's comfortable and stand flat foot tall with who I be.
I ain't the one in search of my identity!

Queendom of Oshun

I carry you in mine eyes.
Sculptured treasure; honey tongued pleasures.
Accented with curry, cayenne pepper,
Initiate thunder; summon mine loving ways.
Bringing forth secrets,
as I cover your mouth
with deep alluring kisses, in answer to your hunger.
Noble intentions spirit you to a safe place.
Mine hands relieve you, with peace on your mind
As I fall upon you like rain.
Seek refuge in mine arms,
comfort between mine breasts.
Your thoughts I am ahead,
as you dine on an appetizing spread.
For all your lifelong grief,
I joyously lay as your relief.
Host dreary thoughts no more.
Lay your love upon me
Soon baby soon,
In the Queendom of Oshun

What Can I Say

What Can I say, Mr. Marvin Gaye
You are missed; as the world turns pandemonium persists
The notion of honor is discharged, drifting afar
Yet, as I witness the escape
I keep pounding and knocking on its door
Hate and misfortunes are running deep
Like Rip Van Winkle humanity is fast asleep

This is more than trouble man
Navigating a world I fail to understand
What can I say, Mr. Marvin Gaye
Eyes wide open
Still can't explain what's going on
More villain politicians
Purposely misfiring upon us
With misdirect directions

Like you, I have to ask what's going on.
Where is the love, where are the leaders, where is humanity?
Ethics on staycation, Moral is bent, Consciousness came and went
Another gun toting stranger on a rampage to kill other strangers
As we pray for a better tomorrow in real time

What can I say, Mr. Marvin Gaye
Brother, sister, mercy me
Our leaders wrapped up in tweets, smart phones, Instagram
Trying to influence through Tik Tok
Moving in shadows on sex-a-phone
As bad actors make a mockery of democracy

What can I say Mr. Marvin Gaye?

Banned From Dunkin Donuts

I love the water, and for nearly two months I rode the ferry from Boston Navy Yard to the Boston Harbor. The ferry was similar to New Orleans except it had a different vibe. This particular day, I exited the ferry, embracing the refreshing breeze. Every morning I'm anxious to walk pass this beautiful building and watch people come and go.

For two weeks I watched the coming and going of people from this particular building. I'm not sure if I were drawn to the building or the construction workers, suits, teenagers, policemen entering and exiting the building. One particular day my curiosity got the better of me; and I followed people into this building.

Imagine my surprise to discover it was just a Dunkin Donuts, but not your typical location; there were no pink signs, no hanging donuts, or coffee cup on this incredible building, with amazing architect.

There I stood in line, as my turn approached, I'd politely let people cut in front of me. The goal was not to buy fried cakes, but; kill time for my activity of people watching. One of the employees was suspiciously watching me, so I departed.

However, I repeated the same routine for several days, my date with Dunkin Donuts were quite enjoyable. One particular day I seemed to have irritated the store manager. People were going about their day, ordering and eating. When this nasal thick voice inquired "Maim, can I help you?" He repeated himself, before I realized that the question was directed at me. I boldly replied "no." He addressed loudly in his Boston accent "Maim, you have been entering my store this past week and haven't bought anything, what can I help you with?" People backed up to distant themselves from me as if I smelled. Mr. Officer of the GD Law continued to sip his coffee causally glancing in my direction.

The manager asked "Who are you?" as if I were some type of spy to steal Dunkin Donuts secret recipes. Simply stating my name was out of the question, and my imagination just swelled with delicious thoughts. In a quiet soft spoken voice, I clearly stated, "I is a runaway slave, searching for a safe house on the Underground Railroad. I is running away from my 6 and 8 year old Massa, those dang on chillin wont me to cook and clean all day. I took the mind to leave them be, and become a fugitive slave. You could literally hear cups hit the floor and liquid splash. Officer of the GD Law and others were choking off their Donuts and Coffee. It was a calmly silence before the stunned customers erupted into laughter.

The manager came from behind the counter with his twisted confrontational managerial face, turned to the officer of the GD Law to inquire what he was going to do. The Officer with this perplexed look stated" what am I going to do, arrest her for being a runaway slave, she has broken no laws?" The manager told me to leave his store and never show my face around there again, as he kindly escorted me out of the door. This is how I was banned from Dunkin Donuts!

We hold on to our youth when we dance with creativity and apply our imagination. For what it's worth, it felt good to live out loud, to be silly me, to laugh and without intent to make others laugh. It only adds to the wonders of this world.

About The Author

Inspired by her upbringing, the author thrives from humble beginnings. Born a Hoosier, raised in Indiana, Mississippi, Louisiana and South Carolina thus nick named Sippianna by her elders. She has a flavor from both the North and the South.

Robin has struggled most of her life to be heard in a world that seems to recognize a standard voice. Still, she has this incredible ability to capture life in the most poetic way.

You are transported through space and time as the author short stories and poetry speaks to the reader. As the Griot, she restores memories of the old way in which you feel love, anger, pain, humor, joy and victory. Her voice is filled with empathy, compassion and truth telling.

White collaborated with four artists from vast and varied backgrounds. Jim Fuge of Durango, Colorado, Ray Skeet of the Navajo Nation in Grand, Canyon, Arizona, James Smith of Helena, Arkansas and Charmaine Neville, of the Neville family, New Orleans, Louisiana.

The author is an agent of change; she hopes to inspire others through her poetry and short stories. Her words of expression and illustrations are thought provoking as you embark on a literary journey, where every page is a new adventure, and every word is a brushstroke on a canvas of emotion.

www.ingramcontent.com/pod-product-compliance
Lightning Source LLC
Chambersburg PA
CBHW020330130626
46549CB00003B/1107